COGNITIVE BEHAVIORAL THERAPY FOR ANXIETY

Master the Negative Voice in Your Head, Change Negative Thoughts, Emotions and Bad Behaviors, Reduce Stress and Anger Management to Overcome Anxiety

John Rich

Table of Contents

Introduction

Anxiety is a troubling experience that is said to affect more than 18% of the global population every single year. With that being said, this number only represents the people who are experiencing problematic anxiety that interferes with their day to day life. The truth is, anxiety can be felt by anyone at any time, no matter who you are or how often you deal with anxiety as a troubling experience. Anxiety itself is actually just a natural emotion, like happiness or sadness. However, anxiety does have the capacity to grow out of control and become seriously problematic in people, which is why so many people might find themselves struggling with problematic anxiety on a regular basis.

If you find that you struggle with anxiety on a regular basis, to the point where it is affecting your day to day life, you need to begin learning new ways to cope with anxiety so that you can reclaim your life. Believe it or not, you do not have to live with problematic anxiety forever, and there are plenty of things that you can do to improve your mental wellness and relieve yourself from chronic anxiety. This is true no matter what type of anxiety you have, so trust that no matter what you are experiencing, there is a solution that can support you in having a higher quality of life.

One of the best solutions that therapists are recommending to this day is cognitive-behavioral therapy or CBT. CBT was introduced back in the 60s but became more popular in the 90s. These days, CBT has been recognized as one of the best natural ways to heal anxiety, amongst other ailments, in people because it focuses less on treating the symptoms and more on treating the root cause of the problem. With that being said, you are still offered incredibly powerful tools to help you overcome the symptoms of anxiety, which means you experience all around relief from the problems you are facing.

If you are looking for a natural way to treat your anxiety, or if you are looking for an opportunity to supplement your existing treatment plan with something more natural to support you in experiencing improved relief, CBT may be just what you are looking for. This method can help you regardless of whether or not you are taking medicines or using any other alternative form of healing as the method has an entirely psychological approach. With that being said, it perfectly complements any existing healing plan you may have in place, or it operates as an excellent healing plan all on its own.

For many, CBT is introduced to them by their therapists, but this does not mean that you need to be in therapy to use or benefit from CBT. This particular technique is actually incredibly simple and easy to apply, which means that you can experience great relief from it, whether you are doing it alone or working with someone else to improve your wellbeing.

Please be sure to take your time as you work through this book so that you can fully understand and implement each practice with intention. The more care you take in focusing on learning and applying each technique, the more likely you will be able to create relief for yourself. If you are ready to learn about what CBT is, how it works, and how you can apply it to yourself to improve and at the same time, treat your anxiety symptoms, let's begin!

Chapter 1: Introducing Cognitive Behavioral Therapy

Cognitive-behavioral therapy is classified as a form of psychotherapy that is used to treat people by changing the way their minds work. In a very basic sense, the purpose is to teach people how to "think they are healthy." The truth is, however, that learning how to use the power of your thoughts to heal your life is incredibly challenging and can take a lot of practice and effort. Having an effective, clear path such as the CBT method and framework can help you apply the power of your thought in a way that actually has the capacity to instill changes in your life.

Before you start learning how to use CBT to help you change your own life through relieving your symptoms of anxiety, it is best that you take the time to know and understand what this is and where it comes from. Whenever you are working on changing your life, especially in a mind-altering way, it is always crucial that you are taking the time to really understand what you are doing and how you are doing it. While CBT is certainly not a dangerous activity, nor does it carry many risks (if any at all), it is still always a good rule of thumb to be intentional about what you are consuming and what treatment methods you are using in your life. Especially when things become problematic, such as anxiety, the situation you are dealing with can become more sensitive, and you need to take extra care to make sure that you are making the best choices for yourself possible.

What is Cognitive Behavioral Therapy (CBT)?

CBT is considered to be a short form of psychotherapy that is used to help people develop skills and strategies that they can use to help them stay more mentally and emotionally healthier in their lives. The goal of CBT is to provide people with adequate coping and resolve skills so that they can stop feeling victimized by their environments and circumstances and start taking control of their lives.

When it comes to CBT, the goal is to find the root cause of your problems and heal them. CBT recognizes that emotions tend to arise from perception and thought, so it often equates the root problem of emotional ailments to thought-based problems that need to be addressed through thought-based solutions. This particular psychotherapy method tends to be more rooted in the present as it cares more about your current problems and symptoms than it does about deep past trauma and memories. When you use CBT, the realization is that while traumas and various highly emotional memories do often serve as the root of a problem, the root lies more deeply in the problems that arise in the brain *after* the trauma, rather than the trauma itself. This trauma can be equated to virtually anything that would stimulate the unhealthy development of emotions that you have been experiencing, such as anxiety, which has to lead you to your desire to seek treatment in the first place.

By being focused on the current situation and how your issues are affecting your present day-to-day life, CBT can offer solutions that will help you reclaim the quality of your life while also bringing closure to the troubles you have experienced. This way, you can begin to experience real change and healing all at the same time.

CBT itself is a structured practice and, when practiced in therapy, usually uses anywhere from 6-20 sessions, but no more. The entire goal is for this particular form of therapy to be short term, effective, and to-the-point so that the individual can get back to living a higher quality of life in a healthier and more complete manner. Each session will be largely focused on identifying problems and creating goals and solutions through learning strategies and skills that will help you reach your goals.

Because of how it works, CBT is powerful in helping heal previous ailments, but it also goes a long way in minimizing or healing from future problems as well because once you have the skills you need to overcome emotional disturbances, they never leave you. In other words, developing an understanding of how to use these techniques will support you with healing now, as well as coping with any future situations because it improves your mental strength and emotional intelligence.

The History of CBT and How it Became Popular

Before CBT was identified as an effective psychotherapy healing method, methods that lead to the creation of CBT existed. These methods were rooted in philosophy in ancient traditions such as Stoicism. Stoic philosophers genuinely believed that logic and reasonable thinking could support someone in identifying and discarding limiting thoughts and beliefs that lead to unwanted emotional experiences. As time went on, researchers began to discover and develop the basis for behavioral therapy, which was the earliest foundation of an entire complex system of behavioral-based psychotherapies that are now used to treat various mental conditions. In the 50s and 60s, behavioral therapies became the focal point of research for many psychologists, and through this, a lot more studies were done to test the effectiveness of this particular treatment method.

Later, in the 80s and 90s, Dr. Aaron T. Beck and Dr. Albert Ellis both took a particular interest in behavioral therapies and how they could be used to support patients in healing their ailments and improving their quality of life. Around the same time, Dr. Beck created CBT, and Dr. Ellis created rational emotive behavior therapy (REBT.) These two therapy methods carry similar structures and beliefs. However, CBT went on to be the most effective and popular one that has been taught to and used by therapists for nearly three decades now.

CBT has gone on to become an "umbrella phrase" for countless types of cognitive-based psychotherapies that are used to help change the minds of people so that they experience less pain and suffering in their lives. Some of the therapies that are blanketed under this phrase are talked about later in this chapter under the section "Alternative Psychotherapies that are Similar to CBT."

The Effectiveness of CBT and What It Can Treat

CBT is considered to be a highly effective cognitive-based psychotherapy that has supported people in overcoming ailments ranging from anxiety and depression to eating disorders and compulsive behaviors. Because of how CBT works, it has proven to have high effectiveness in helping people change their minds by creating new neural pathways that lead to new ways of thinking, believing, feeling, and behaving in their lives.

The entire method of CBT is based on the understanding that the human brain has a select series of biases that contribute to how it automatically perceives and thinks about reality. This means that every single one of us is predisposed to seeing our world through a certain lens, so to speak. If your lens is somehow off or supporting an unrealistic, unhelpful, or false perspective that is leading to you feeling anxious, depressed, or any other particularly intense and unhelpful emotion, chances are it is not serving you. Rather than living the rest of your life feeling "doomed" to being trapped in this one viewpoint, you can use CBT to essentially change your lens so that you can see life in a different light.

Once people change their cognitive lens or cognitive framework as it is often called in CBT, they find themselves feeling free from ailments like anxiety, depression, and otherwise. This is because they have officially broken down the methods of perceiving, thinking, and believing that they were leading to feelings and behaviors that were unhelpful to the individual.

Across the world, there have been hundreds of thousands of people who have successfully engaged in CBT and seen massive improvements in their ailments. Some go on to completely recover from their ailments, whereas others go on to find themselves feeling far more in control, so they are no longer at risk of having such intense symptoms. With that being said, it is important to understand that sometimes there are incredibly complex cases of anxiety, depression, or other disorders that may not benefit from CBT alone. If you find yourself falling into the category of a highly complex scenario, you may find that you need to combine CBT with other treatments, therapies, or even medicines to help you seek relief from your ailments. There are no right or wrong answers, just the ones that help you feel better, so make sure that you take this into consideration and create a treatment plan with your team that best serves your needs.

Alternative Psychotherapies that are Similar to CBT

As I previously mentioned, CBT is often used as an umbrella term for many different types of cognitive-based psychotherapies at this point. Often, people who are engaging in CBT will engage in elements of other cognitive-based psychotherapies, too, so that they can experience complete relief from their ailments. With that being said, it might be helpful to recognize what these different forms of treatment are so that you have a clear understanding of what other avenues you might want to look at and educate yourself on when it comes to treating your own ailments.

The other treatment methods include REBT, acceptance, and commitment therapy (ACT), dialectical behavior therapy (DBT), reality therapy/choice therapy, cognitive processing therapy, EMDR, and multimodal therapy.

Rational Emotive Behavior Therapy (REBT)

The focus of REBT is to take an active-directive approach in healing yourself by recognizing your problematic thoughts and behaviors and directing yourself in a new direction. The practice also revolves around learning about emotional intelligence so that you can learn to navigate your emotions in a healthier and more intentional manner, allowing you to experience greater relief from troubling beliefs and emotions.

Acceptance and Commitment Therapy (ACT)

Acceptance and commitment therapy (ACT) focuses on teaching people to accept what is and what has already happened and commit to finding ways to move forward and heal from their past. The goal of ACT is to prevent people from mourning too long or clinging to the past due to an inability to commit to letting the past go and moving forward with their lives. With ACT, you essentially set the commitment that you will move forward no matter what.

Dialectical Behavior Therapy (DBT)

The goal of dialectical behavior therapy (DBT) focuses largely on helping people improve their mindfulness, distress tolerance, emotion regulation, and interpersonal effectiveness so that they can have healthier relationships with themselves and others. The goal is to stop having traumatic or overwhelming relations with other people so that the individual can begin managing their own emotions and experiences in difficult situations more effectively. It is most effective in treating things like a borderline personality disorder.

Reality Therapy/Choice Therapy

Reality therapy (RT) or choice therapy, as it is sometimes called, is a form of therapy that focuses on helping people identify what is truly real, take responsibility for themselves and their reality, and learn to navigate life with a clear understanding of right from wrong. The goal is to prevent people from suffering from the inability to attain their basic needs by helping them root themselves in the present and in reality and commit to taking care of themselves and their wellbeing through intentional choice.

Cognitive Processing Therapy (CPT)

Cognitive processing therapy (CPT) is used to help people focus on healing from things like post-traumatic stress disorder and other related conditions that are caused by trauma. This particular therapy uses elements of CBT in a more refined way that is focused more exclusively on healing trauma, rather than healing generalized ailments like anxiety or depression. Essentially, the big difference is that it is focused on massive, deep, and often heavy traumas that people are facing in their lives.

Eye Movement Desensitization and Reprocessing (EMDR)

Eye movement desensitization and reprocessing (EMDR) is rooted in the belief that your eyes move in specific directions when you are being asked to recall various events in your life, or create new realities in your life. In other words, memories cause certain eye movements, and creating stories cause different eye movements. The idea is that you can begin to rewire your brain and change your conscious and subconscious mind by intentionally changing the direction of your eye movements as you tell traumatic stories from your past. In doing so, you rewire your brain and desensitize yourself to the content of your traumatic memories and experiences.

Chapter 2: How Cognitive Behavioral Therapy Works

Now that you know what CBT is and how it came to be used for healing various ailments, you are probably wondering more about the practice itself. For example, you might wonder what it is exactly or how it works. With a strong understanding of how CBT came to be and where it came from, you are now ready to understand exactly how it works, the framework that CBT is developed with, and how that framework shifts from ailment to ailment.

What we are about to cover in this chapter essentially walks you through the foundation of what a trained therapist or psychologist would walk you through if you were engaging in CBT with them. This way, you have a clear understanding of what the path is that you will be taking to heal yourself and how you can apply that path to various ailments in your life.

Note that in this chapter, we are going to explore CBT more along the lines of what this particular psychotherapy looks like in general. This way, you can understand the basic framework of what CBT actually is and how this framework can be applied to healing multiple different mental disorders and conditions. Later, in Chapter 5, we will explore how this particular framework is applied to anxiety.

How Does CBT Work?

Cognitive behavioral therapy has a six-phase approach to helping people heal their mental conditions that they are dealing with. The goal is to recognize cognitive distortions that they are experiencing and identify ways that they can overcome these cognitive distortions by ultimately creating stronger coping methods, cognition, emotions, and behaviors. The goal is to create people who are more adaptive and capable of being involved in the real world with less problematic experiences in their emotions and cognitions.

The entire cycle of CBT starts with recognizing what the problematic behaviors and experiences are and using those to identify the problematic cycles that people are facing in their minds, which lead to these behaviors and experiences. After that, the individual learns CBT-based techniques that are meant to help them navigate those thoughts, feelings, and behaviors in a healthy and more effective manner. Through that, they are able to begin changing their problematic cycles, which results in them experiencing newer, less troubling cycles in their lives.

As time goes on, the individual may find the need for new coping skills as they face new challenges in their lives. However, the general idea is that the coping skills offered in the original CBT treatment will support them in having an easier time recognizing the need for new skills and ultimately developing them on their own or, with minimal support from a therapist if they feel it is needed.

Basic CBT Framework

CBT relies on a basic framework that follows six phases. These six phases are meant to draw a map for how the individual is going to get from where they are now to where they want to be. This entire forward-focus of CBT is what leads to individuals having such a great benefit from CBT as it supports them with coping and healing going forward, rather than placing excessive emphasis on what has happened in the past. For many people, the troubles lie less in what has happened and more in how that has affected their everyday way of life and their future if they do not regain control over the problems they have been facing.

The six phases outlined in the CBT framework include assessment, reconceptualization, skills acquisition, skills consolidation and application, generalization and maintenance, and post-treatment assessment.

Phase One: Assessment

The first phase in CBT is to assess what the problem is and get a full scope understanding of what this problem is leading to an individual's life. The idea is to create a map of sorts that shows where the problem is starting and what it is leading to every single time it takes place. Often in this phase, people see that their problems are leading to situations that are causing more of the same problem to keep occurring. This can lead to people feeling like they are "stuck" or like there is no way for them to escape the cycle that they are living in, and so they seek treatment.

Getting a full and clear understanding of what the problem is and what the problem entails is important, as this is the entire foundation upon which the individual will be able to begin changing their experiences. You need to make sure that you have everything in place and clearly understood so that you can identify the proper strategies that are going to support you in healing the ailments that have caused you to seek treatment in the first place.

Phase Two: Reconceptualization

The next part of the CBT framework is reconceptualization. Often, once people identify the cycles of their problems, they realize that in their minds, they feel as though things could not possibly go in any other way. The idea is that the way things are now is unchangeable and that people will always continue to have these experiences and feel this way and that there is nothing that can be done about it. Of course, this very set of beliefs leads to them feeling trapped in the first place because they are incapable of seeing that there are other possibilities for how things could go or what could be done to break the cycle.

During the reconceptualization phase, the entire purpose is to identify what can be changed about the individual's present belief system to make one that is far more supportive of their goals in life. This way, they can begin to see beyond their limited perspective and limiting beliefs and start to see into a new truth or a new way of thinking that supports them in breaking the cycle. In some cases, the belief shift is slight, whereas, on others, an entirely new way of perceiving and believing may be required to help the person completely move on from that way of behaving.

Phase Three: Skills Acquisition

Now that the individual has identified the new goals and new way of perceiving their reality, they need to move into acquiring skills that can help them actually reinforce these new beliefs in their life. Often, people do not believe a different way of life because they do not have the skills needed actually to make that way of life exist, so they believe that they are incapable of getting there. When you begin to create the skills, you need to have the reality you want to have, believing that it is possible and getting there becomes a lot easier. As well, changing your mind becomes a lot easier, too, because you are no longer feeling trapped within your cycles, and instead, you start having hope for what you can experience in the future.

Understand that the phase of actually acquiring skills is more about identifying what skills would help you improve your situation and learning about how to apply those skills to your everyday life. The actual process of applying your skills to your ailment that has led to you seeking treatment in the first place is a two-step process that requires you first to acquire and practice the skills you have discovered.

Phase Four: Skills Consolidation and Application

After you have discovered what skills are going to work best for you when it comes to treating your ailment, and you have practiced them, you need to begin consolidating them and applying them toward your actual ailment. This is the part of your process where you get the opportunity to bring these skills all together into one treatment and use them to help you change your mind completely.

As you begin to consolidate your skills, you need to identify how you can reasonably apply them to your ability to overcome your ailment. This means that you need to go back to the map you drew out in phase one and identify where these skills would best be used, then prepare yourself for those circumstances by identifying how and when you are going to apply your new skills. Once you have created these expectations around yourself and your treatment, you can begin to actually implement your new skills in these areas and allow yourself to begin experiencing the benefits of them.

When it comes to CBT, this is often the part that takes the longest as it can be challenging to adapt to new ways of thinking and behaving in emotionally charged settings. There are several ways that you can improve this part of the process and make it easier, ranging from exposure therapy to focusing more on building the skills before implementing them for your initial ailment.

Phase Five: Generalization and Maintenance

After you have begun routinely applying your new skills to your particular ailment, the next phase is to focus on generalization and maintenance. This is the part of CBT, where you begin to learn how to take these new skills and strategies and turn them into actual routine practices that you are going to apply to your life as a habit. This is how you can begin to embrace your changes in a way that is more automatic.

In addition to embracing your changes in a habitual way for your existing ailments, you also want to learn how to generalize these skills so that you can use them for many areas of your life. Since CBT largely focuses on stress management and stress response, these techniques can be used in many ways for people. Learning how to generalize your skills and apply them to multiple areas of your life can be helpful in minimizing your present ailment while also supporting yourself in experiencing a healthier life overall.

Phase Six: Post-Treatment Assessment

As you continue to apply your CBT treatment to your ailment, you need to make sure that you take the time to perform a post-treatment assessment to see if your new skills are actually helping you or not. Your post-treatment assessment will be done many times over until the point where you find that you have experienced significant enough relief for an extended period of time, which ultimately proves that you are no longer struggling.

It is important to understand that even when your assessment says you are "all better," you still need to implement and reinforce your new skills. If you revert back to your old way of living and experiencing immediately after this realization, you will find yourself experiencing tremendous struggles in your life as you face difficulties in your way of coping once again. You must always continue to embrace your new way of being so that you can continue to overcome the problematic ailment while also preventing the development of any future problematic ailments due to poor coping methods.

Chapter 3: Understanding the Implications of Anxiety

As you learn to cope with anxiety, it is important to understand how anxiety is implicating your life clearly. Many people recognize that they live with anxiety but do not realize how many aspects of their lives are actively being affected by their anxiety. The reality is that anxiety actually has a much bigger impact than most people realize, and taking the time to understand the impact and implications of anxiety will help you understand how you can begin to support yourself in overcoming *all* of your anxiety symptoms. This way, you will be far more likely to relieve yourself of all of your anxiety symptoms so that you can experience life without any anxiety or any problematic anxiety symptoms.

What Does Anxiety Look and Feel Like?

The way anxiety looks and feels largely depends on what type of anxiety you are facing, and what stage you are at in your development. For example, a child experiencing anxiety is going to look a lot different from an adult experiencing anxiety. Likewise, someone experiencing acute anxiety or generalized anxiety disorder is going to look a lot different from someone experiencing obsessive-compulsive disorder or post-traumatic stress syndrome.

Despite the many differences that occur that can impact the way anxiety looks and feels, the general core experience and the image are fairly similar from person to person. It is recognizing what anxiety looks and feels like it can help you identify anxiety within yourself while also being able to identify it in others as well, possibly. While it is not your job or duty to identify anxiety in others, at times being able to do so can help you behave in a more compassionate, gentle, and mindful manner toward another person who may be suffering or struggling.

When you yourself are the person experiencing any form of anxiety disorder, the number one thing that seems to appear in everyone is a chronic worry. People with anxiety disorders of any variety find themselves constantly worrying about what other people are thinking, what is going to happen, or how they are going to be able to navigate their lives. Often, people with anxiety will find themselves worrying to the point that they begin to worry excessively about things that are not particularly important or that do not require such a massive amount of worry in the first place. For example, rather than being slightly concerned that you will be late for work if you hit traffic, you might begin to experience massive worry to the point where you begin to jump to worst-case scenarios, such as believing that you will be fired on the spot for being late.

This chronic level of overwhelming worry seems to exist in everyone with any form of anxiety, although the context and severity of the worry vary from person to person. Likewise, the actual symptoms that accompany the worry tend to vary from person to person, too. You could find yourself experiencing anything from fidgeting and discomfort to cold sweats, tremors, and even feeling as though your legs are too numb for you to stand up and walk to go do whatever you need to get done. You may even find yourself having trouble sleeping, concentrating, or staying alert in various situations because your mind constantly feels tired and overwhelmed from all of the worryings.
Something that is often quite unexpected yet incredibly common for anxiety disorders is also the presence of anger and irritability. Oftentimes, people who have been struggling with anxiety disorder claim that they feel easily angered or irritated, yet they may not know why or how to explain it. Believe it or not, this is actually incredibly common for people with anxiety as it is caused by them having a heightened fight or flight response, which can sometimes lead them into the "fight" response if they feel the need to.

For this reason, if you find yourself or someone you know experiencing chronic and overwhelming anger, chances are what they are actually experiencing intense anxiety. This is why many psychologists and psychiatrists say that anger is a secondary emotion: because it is typically caused by an underlying emotion such as fear or anxiety.

Symptoms of Anxiety

There are many different symptoms that fall into the category of anxiety because of how many anxiety disorders actually exist. With that being said, there are some common symptoms that everyone seems to experience regardless of what their unique type of anxiety actually is. We are going to start by identifying what the common and core symptoms of anxiety are first so that you can begin to pinpoint and understand your own anxiety disorder. Then, in the next section, we will go into different types of anxiety and anxiety disorders and what additional symptoms you might experience if you have a more specific disorder, as opposed to a generalized disorder.

The common and core symptoms of anxiety are often recognized as twelve different symptoms that seem to be present in all or most people who experience anxiety. Chances are, you experience at least half of these in your own life if you have anxiety, too.

The twelve common or core symptoms of anxiety include:
- Overwhelming feelings of worry, nervousness, restlessness, or being tense;
- Feeling as though there is impending danger, panic, or doom;
- Hyperventilation (rapid breathing rate);
- Increased heart rate;
- Trembling;
- Sweating;
- Feeling weak or feeling suddenly and overwhelmingly tired;
- Having difficulty concentrating or redirecting your thoughts;
- Difficulty sleeping;
- Gastrointestinal problems like indigestion, nausea, or irritable bowel syndrome;
- Difficulty controlling worried thoughts and feelings;
- Constantly trying to avoid the triggers that cause anxiety.

These symptoms are not the only symptoms, although they do tend to be exceedingly common in virtually everyone who experiences anxiety, no matter what type of anxiety disorder they are dealing with. Learning how to acknowledge and cope with these symptoms in your life will help you begin to overcome anxiety so that you are less likely to experience so much overwhelm and struggle in your own life.

Different Types of Anxiety and Anxiety Disorders

In addition to knowing what the core symptoms of anxiety are, it can also be helpful to identify different types of anxiety and anxiety disorders. Finding out exactly what you are struggling with and how it is affecting your everyday life can give you even more of an opportunity to overcome it so that you are no longer struggling with these symptoms. As well, sometimes, certain specific disorders require specific treatments or considerations to avoid you possibly worsening your anxiety or struggling longer than you need to.

There are ten different unique anxiety disorders that you should be aware of, although they may exist, so these are not the only disorders you need to consider. If you feel that you have an anxiety disorder but do not see it listed here, it can be helpful to talk to a general care practitioner or a psychiatrist to seek help in identifying what you may be dealing with.

The ten different anxiety disorders to be aware of include: agoraphobia, medical-caused anxiety disorder, generalized anxiety disorder, panic disorder, selective mutism, separation anxiety disorder, social anxiety disorder, specific phobias, substance-induced anxiety disorder, and other specified and unspecified disorders.

Agoraphobia

Agoraphobia is a form of anxiety disorder that is characterized by people who are afraid of situations and places that cause them to feel anxious or overwhelmed. Often, if a person feels trapped, helpless, embarrassed, or like they are too far removed from their "safety," they will begin to experience massive anxiety. Agoraphobia is most often recognized in people who avoid or refuse to leave their homes, especially to go to a place that they deem uncomfortable or unsafe.

Medical-Caused Anxiety Disorder

In some cases, people who are experiencing health problems may find themselves experiencing a medical-caused anxiety disorder. This ultimately means that anxiety is being caused by the other condition they are facing, likely because it is affecting their nervous system, hormones, or the chemicals within their body. The key to healing this type of anxiety will lie in treating the root cause while also treating problematic anxiety symptoms through means such as CBT to ensure that they do not last longer than necessary.

Generalized Anxiety Disorder

The most common form of anxiety disorder out there is a generalized anxiety disorder, and it is characterized by persistent and excessive worry about activities or events, even ones that people are used to. For example, you might experience massive ongoing anxiety about going to work every day, even though you have been going to the same job every day for years now. Often, people with this disorder struggle to change their emotions and find their anxiety affecting their physical wellness, too. This particular form of anxiety is often found in people who are also struggling with depression.

Panic Disorder

Some people experience a form of anxiety disorder that involves them feeling sudden and overwhelming feelings of anxiety and fear that leads to intense terror and the outbreak of panic attacks. These panic attacks peak within minutes and then often disappear fairly quickly, too, although some people may experience the attack for around an hour and may experience the "come down" for up to four hours after as their body recovers. This disorder often comes with shortness of breath, a rapid heartbeat, chest pain, and feelings of impending doom. Often, people who experience panic disorder aggressively avoid the triggers that cause them and live in intense fear that they will happen again.

Selective Mutism

This particular anxiety disorder is most common in children and is represented by a consistent failure to speak in certain situations. For example, they may fail to speak in school despite being able to speak perfectly fine at home or with close friends. This particular type of anxiety disorder is often caused by being uncomfortable or feeling out of place in new situations, which can lead to children becoming extremely introverted. Whether it is experienced in childhood or adulthood, it can lead to interferences in school, work, and social situations.

Separation Anxiety Disorder

Separation anxiety disorder also tends to exist mostly in childhood, although it can occur in adulthood, too, especially as a secondary disorder accompanying something like post-traumatic stress disorder. Separation anxiety essentially means that you begin to experience massive and overwhelming anxiety when you are separated from someone. In children, this often comes from being separated from your parents or parent-like figures. In adulthood, it may exist in any close form of relationship, such as one you might share with your spouse or if you have a care aide for a certain illness, one you might experience when they leave.

Social Anxiety Disorder

Social anxiety disorder is also known as social phobia, and it is characterized by people who struggle with being in social situations due to high levels of anxiety. These individuals may experience fear, embarrassment, excessive self-consciousness, or excessive worry about being judged by other people in social settings. If you find yourself avoiding social situations and feeling overwhelmed when you are in them, you may be experiencing a social anxiety disorder.

Specific Phobias

Specific phobias can be developed around just about anything, so it is hard to focus on one area. Instead, psychologists and psychiatrists often see phobias as being something that manifests similarly in anyone who experiences phobias. Specific phobias often invoke the occurrence of panic attacks in people who are exposed to the phobia and can be incredibly overwhelming and even life-altering. People who have specific phobias often completely avoid the thing that they are experiencing a phobia toward.

Substance-Induced Anxiety Disorder

Substance-induced anxiety disorder can be caused when people experience anxiety as a result of misusing drugs, or when they are taking medications. It can also occur when they are exposed to a toxic substance or when they experience withdrawal from drugs if they have been misusing drugs in their lives. This particular anxiety disorder often only arises around the use of medications or drugs and tends to subside when the individual stops taking them or misusing them, depending on what the scenario is. With that being said, if a person has been misusing drugs and begins to experience anxiety around the withdrawal, it will take much longer for their anxiety symptoms to subside as they will have to wait out the withdrawal period.

Other Specified and Unspecified Disorders

Sometimes, people experience anxiety disorders or phobias that do not necessarily fit within any of the aforementioned categories or criteria. As a result, doctors consider these individuals to have other specified or unspecified disorders. If they can identify what is causing the disorder and what problems exist around it, they are called specified disorders. If they cannot identify what is causing the disorder, they are often called unspecified disorders. Often, specified and unspecified disorders are significant enough to be distressing and disruptive still, which is why people seek treatment for them in the first place.

The Causes of Anxiety

Anxiety itself can be caused by many things, so identifying the exact cause of anxiety can be slightly difficult. If you already have a suspicion of what your anxiety has been caused by, chances are you are feeling pretty clear and aware of why you are dealing with your symptoms. If, however, you are not clear on why you are dealing with your symptoms, it may be particularly frustrating and overwhelming to realize that you are experiencing them and that you do not seem to have any known cause or reason behind why you are experiencing them.

In general, anxiety can be caused by three things: an acute experience, an ongoing experience, or a medical experience. Identifying which of these categories your anxiety fits into will help you understand the occurrence of your anxiety and what is causing it to exist within your own life.

Acute Experience

An acute onset of anxiety is caused by a specific event resulting in an individual to feel traumatized or overwhelmed, which leads to the development of anxiety in your life. These experiences often lead to things like phobias or panic disorders, though they may also lead to the development of generalized anxiety depending on what you faced and how it is manifesting in your unique life.

If you experience the acute onset of anxiety, it is often easy to tell why. These onsets are typically easily recalled by the individual experiencing anxiety and tend to continue to come to mind anytime the person experiences anxiety. For example, if you got in a car accident, you might find yourself feeling intense anxiety around cars and when driving cars. Or, if you were in an abusive relationship, you might find yourself experiencing anxiety within relationships in your life.

Sometimes, acute causes for anxiety are things that are seemingly small to an individual, yet they have an incredibly powerful impact on that person's psyche and emotional experiences. I explain more of why this happens in my book *Emotional Intelligence for Self-Discipline*. However, the easiest way to explain it is this: your subconscious is responsible for recognizing and remembering all of your feelings. If you find yourself feeling extremely distressed over something, even over something seemingly small, like a spider being on your bed or a mouse crawling across your counter, it can cause an intense experience for your subconscious mind. As a result, your subconscious mind might translate that into a phobia and begin to produce strong feelings of overwhelm and anxiety every time you see, talk about, or hear about spiders or mice.

Ongoing Experience

Ongoing experiences that lead to the development of anxiety can sometimes be the hardest experiences to identify because they are rarely chalked down to any one thing. Ongoing experiences can include experiencing overwhelming stress at work, feeling overworked or neglected at home, and feeling irritated every time you drive anywhere. You might find yourself feeling annoyed with having to visit doctor's appointments or go to your kid's recital, or any other number of things because they cause overwhelm in your schedule or in your life experience. Often, it is a ton of little things that build up over time that lead to an individual feeling overwhelmed and, eventually, anxious.

This type of situation most commonly leads to generalized anxiety disorder because it leads to the person experiencing anxiety, worry, and overwhelm in every area of their lives. Often, if you experience anxiety from this root cause, you will find yourself jumping to the worst conclusion in every way possible. You might find yourself worrying about your drive to work, your ability to please your partner, your abilities as a parent, or your worthiness as a person in general. You may often find yourself feeling like everything bad is going to happen, and like you are the root cause and that no matter what you try, you are not going to be able to stop yourself from experiencing this level of overwhelm and uncertainty.

Many people do not realize that the modern way of living life is not necessarily the most nurturing to our mental health. If you are experiencing a "typical" life and you are not taking the time to nurture yourself and your wellbeing, you are going to find yourself experiencing intense overwhelm and anxiety and possibly depression as well. Modern-day living requires important and mandatory self-care practices such as time off, extra time spent resting, and other emotionally and mentally nurturing activities to avoid the constant stress leading to mental and emotional disorders.

Medical Experience

If you experience a medically-caused anxiety disorder, then it is only natural to realize that your anxiety is being caused by a medical experience. Medical experiences can cause anxiety disorders when they affect the nervous system, hormones, or chemicals in your body in any way. There is a massive list of different illnesses and conditions ranging from infections and treatable illnesses and injuries to untreatable and chronic illnesses that can lead to depression. If you have or suspect that you have a medical condition that is causing you to experience anxiety, you need to talk to your doctor to identify what you can do to help yourself stop experiencing anxiety as a result of these conditions.

Often, medically-induced anxiety can be treated by identifying and healing the root cause of the anxiety. With that being said, that is not always the case. Some chronic or untreatable illnesses will attack the central nervous system or the hormones and chemicals within someone's body and, therefore, cannot be treated. Instead, they are often managed with anxiety and coping methods like CBT or other cognitive-based psychotherapy options that support the individual in feeling more nurtured and cared for.

Chapter 4: Identifying Your Need to Heal

For some people, identifying the difference between regular anxiety and problematic anxiety may be somewhat challenging. Often, when we are facing troubling experiences within our minds, we may either minimize them or make them worse through the way in which we think about them. Naturally, neither of these is ideal as they can prevent you from realistically assessing what you are dealing with and creating a reasonable path for you to heal as you go forward.

As you begin to face healing your anxiety, you are going to need to identify what you are dealing with accurately, and you need to heal. The more you can accurately understand what you are in need of, the easier it is going to be for you to honestly face your anxiety and begin to heal yourself from it.

Understanding When Anxiety has Become Problematic

Understanding when your anxiety has reached the point of problematic may be easy, or it may be challenging, depending on who you are. Some people have a personality that is naturally more likely to recognize and accept when things have become too challenging, whereas others might find themselves wanting to pretend nothing is wrong or truly believing nothing is wrong. In addition to personality, making it hard for people to accept that they are dealing with troubling anxiety symptoms, stigmas surrounding mental illness, and anxiety can also make it challenging. This is said to be especially true for males who are dealing with anxiety, as males are typically challenged to "man up" rather than accept when they are dealing with troubling emotional experiences.

If you find that you are having difficulties identifying whether or not your anxiety has become problematic, there are a few things that you can do to begin to identify whether or not your anxiety is truly troubling you. The first thing you need to consider is this: if you are reading this book, you can already feel confident that your anxiety is troubling you enough to seek help. In this case, this means that your anxiety is more than a little bothersome and that you are dealing with anxiety that needs to be addressed with some form of treatment. At this point, it is more about identifying *how* troublesome your anxiety has become so that you can get an honest assessment of what you are dealing with and what you need to do and expect when it comes to treating your anxiety.

The reality is that anxiety becomes problematic the minute you stop being able to control it, and you start experiencing it on a consistent basis. Natural, healthy anxiety is something that should only be experienced during situations where you would expect that you might feel a burst of anxiety. For example, if you are getting up on stage to talk to a crowd of people or if you just narrowly missed a car accident when you were merging onto a fast road. In these scenarios, anxiety would be expected, and your anxious response would be normal. In fact, having a certain amount of lingering anxiety following these events would be normal, too.

If, however, you find that your anxiety is repeatedly being triggered by seemingly small things, there is a possibility that you are experiencing problematic anxiety. This type of anxiety can be incredibly challenging to face, as it can lead to you experiencing excessive and repeated worries over things that are beyond your control. Often, it can also lead to excessive and repeated worries over small things that do not seem to be worthy of any level of anxiety, either.

Often, problematic anxiety is deemed as being irrational, and in most instances, the person dealing with the anxiety recognizes that their fears and concerns are irrational, too. Still, they tend to find themselves feeling as though the anxiety is incredibly real, and they struggle to regain control over their emotions because it seems as though they have taken over control, and they are no longer able to manage their emotions on their own. In emotional intelligence terms, this is called *emotional hijacking.*

If you find that your own anxiety tends to be irrational, or that you find your anxiety being triggered multiple times a day, or multiple times a week to levels that feel hard to manage, chances are you are dealing with problematic anxiety. In this case, you need to find a way for you to navigate your anxiety in a healthier manner so that you are no longer facing the troubles that come with problematic anxiety.

Recognizing That There is A Life Beyond Anxiety

When you realize that your anxiety has become problematic, it can be easy to think that there is no hope for you ever to be able to live a normal life after this realization. Many people believe that they will have to spend the rest of their lives, answering to anxiety and feeling washed over by moments of panic, worry, and excessive nerves. Learning how to navigate your life with anxiety may seem challenging, to the point where you may not believe that there is a life beyond anxiety.

It is important to understand that anxiety is not a lifelong sentence and that, yes, you are having problems right now, but these problems are not bound to last forever. Anxiety can often be healed and managed in a way that allows the individual suffering never to have to deal with problematic anxiety again. And, when it can't be, strong skills can be learned that help you deal with your anxiety in a more intentional and powerful way. As a result, you are less likely to find yourself facing the traumatic experiences of having unmanaged anxiety.

As you begin to navigate the process of managing your anxiety, it is crucial that you keep an open mind and stay hopeful that there is a way for you to experience a more positive life without so much anxiety. One big mistake people tend to make involves closing themselves off and believing that there is no hope for them and that they are incapable of creating any changes in their lives. When you believe that there is nothing to be done and that you are bound to suffer for the rest of your life, what you do is you close your mind completely to your ability actually to make any changes to your emotional and thought-based experiences. As a result, your subconscious mind also believes this to be true and begins to struggle with the idea of ever allowing change to take root in your mind truly.

If you are going to be able to manage and cope with your anxiety in a healthy manner, you are going to need to be able to keep an open mind. This way, you stay willing and receptive to the changes that you have the power to make within yourself, and you actually put effort into creating and maintaining the skills that will help you navigate and manage your anxiety on a day to day basis. As long as you remain consistent and you keep practicing with your ability to stay open and use the skills that you are learning about, you will likely be able to have a massive and lasting impact on your ability to manage your anxiety.

Becoming Willing to Face Your Anxiety, Phobias, and Traumas

Becoming willing to face your anxiety, phobias, and traumas are about more than just keeping an open mind, although an open mind is important. In addition to an open mind, you need to realize that actually managing and facing your anxiety, phobias, or traumas is going to require you to be able to face them. Understand that all forms of therapy, including CBT, are going to require you to become present with your anxieties, phobias, and traumas enough to be able to heal them and navigate them in a new way. If you are too afraid to face them, then you are not going to be able to do what it takes for you to be able to build and execute the strategies and skills associated with therapies and treatments like CBT.

Although CBT is a forward-thinking form of therapy, it does require you to acknowledge what your anxieties, phobias, and traumas are so that you can put yourself in front of them and navigate them on purpose. If you are too unwilling to face your anxieties, you are going to find yourself struggling to acquire and enforce the skills to overcome them because you will not be able to change the cycle.

It may be scary to become willing to face your anxieties, especially if you have an intense amount of fear and panic built around them. If you have been living with them for quite some time, the idea of facing them and overcoming them may sound both scary and impossible as you may feel as though you have already tried so hard to do this in the past, and now you are being asked to do it again. Trust, however, that if you are going to be able to heal yourself from your anxiety, then you are going to need to be to face your anxiety. This includes facing the experiences or memories that raise anxiety within you so that you can change the cycles as they play out.

One important thing to remember when you are becoming willing to face your anxieties is this: if you never face them, they will always exist. Even though you may be able to avoid them and look the other way in most cases, you might find yourself unexpectedly coming across them and having more traumatic experiences as you go forward. Each time this cycle plays out, your anxiety will increase, and you may find that anxiety leaking further and further into other areas of your life, ultimately causing even less quality of life in your life. If you take the time to address your anxieties, however, it can be scary to face them, but as you do, you will realize that you can actually face them intentionally and in a way that makes them feel less and less bothersome each time.

Understand, too, that facing your anxieties on your own terms also means that you can control the rate at which you face them. This way, rather than being excessively exposed and overwhelmed all in one go, you can find ways to gradually increase your exposure over time so that you feel as though you have more control in every situation. Then, since you are in control, you may find that you naturally feel less anxious as you go anyway.

Chapter 5: Cognitive Behavioral Therapy and Anxiety

CBT is an amazing psychotherapy that you can use to treat many different mental and emotional conditions, including anxiety. If you are dealing with anxiety, learning how to use and apply CBT to your life properly can help you create stronger skills and strategies to overcome anxiety as well as any other emotional or mental condition you may face in your life. CBT, in general, can support people in having a healthier sense of emotional intelligence, which makes navigating your troubles much easier, no matter how big or small they may seem. People who tend to get the most benefit from CBT recognize that the skills work in a variety of different situations and make an effort to apply them in a variety of different situations, too.

Despite the fact that CBT has a consistent framework, no matter what ailment you may be treated with it, there are certain unique aspects that exist when treating anxiety. These unique aspects reside within CBT itself, as well as within your unique approach, the goals you might set, and the experiences and emotions you might face as you are undertaking the process of actually achieving your goals with CBT. Learning how to prepare yourself for these things can help you navigate CBT and your anxiety much more clearly so that you can create a stronger impact on your treatment method.

How CBT Works in Healing Anxiety

CBT works with anxiety, specifically by helping you recognize and intercept the thoughts that are causing you to find your way to anxious spirals. The idea behind this is that your thoughts are responsible for causing your anxious spirals. Each time you are surrounded by an environment or circumstances that trigger you, you create perceptions that cause thoughts and beliefs around what you believe to be true. Through these thoughts and beliefs, you find yourself developing feelings as well as a way to support you in navigating your reality. As a result, you are able to create the necessary levels of energy, attention, and other physiological responses to help you engage in your environment.

When you are experiencing problematic anxiety, the understanding is that this entire process of developing emotions is being affected by the perception that you are in some way not safe, or that something bad is going to happen. When you find yourself feeling as though something bad is going to happen, you find yourself immediately digging deeper into feelings of worry, which results in feelings of anxiety. The problem really lies in situations where you are perceiving danger and creating anxiety when no real threat exists. If you find yourself experiencing anxiety on a consistent basis, especially when you do not see a reason for you to feel anxious, chances are you are creating anxiety within yourself based on what you perceive to be true about your environment.

If you can identify what your perceptions are, recognize where your perceptions are wrong, and adjust your perceptions with intentional mindfulness and mindful behaviors, you can actually intercept and stop your anxiety in many instances. The key that you really need to understand in all of this, however, is that what you are doing is working on changing your subconscious habits, which is not necessarily an easy thing to do. For this reason, you may engage in the practice of CBT many times over before you begin to experience significant relief. Often, people who engage in CBT find themselves feeling hopeful and recognizing the potential for change early on, but not really experiencing significant lasting change until they have enforced their new practices a few times over. Once they have, they find themselves feeling a lot more hopeful and significantly improved symptoms from what they had experienced in the past.

Aside from being consistent and being willing to keep trying until you find your way through, it is also important to understand that a large part of CBT's effectiveness resides in the skills and strategies that you are going to learn along the way. The skills and strategies that you learn will directly affect your ability to navigate anxiety more effectively. This means that the focus you use when building these skills will be unique to your goals around anxiety, and they will be focused on helping you navigate anxiety more effectively so that you can improve your ability to create change in your life.

The CBT Framework for Anxiety

The CBT framework for anxiety is easy to understand, although navigating it can be more challenging because you will be in the midst of navigating some intense emotions along the way. In fact, these strong emotions are why CBT strives to remain as simple as possible: so that you do not have to attempt to understand many different complex strategies and practices during intense emotional periods. The more simple you can keep this in your mind, and your life, the more effective it is going to be when it comes time for you to heal from your anxiety.

The first thing you are going to do when you begin dealing with your anxiety with CBT is acknowledging where you are at and understanding your existing anxiety cycles. You need to know what you are dealing with, especially on a mental and emotional level, if you are going to be able to overcome your anxiety and create more room for growth along the way. If you cannot get clear on what you are dealing with or what is going on in your mind at the time of you experiencing anxiety, you are going to have a hard time making any changes in your life because you will not necessarily understand what needs your attention and what needs to be changed.

Next, you are going to start looking for ways to actually change the map so that you can start intentionally creating a new cycle for yourself. At this point, you are only going to be spotting the problematic area of your existing cycle and then mapping out what you are going to do instead. This part is actually a two-step part of the process that starts with you identifying what the problem is and then leads into you identifying what you are going to do about it and what skills you need to help you get there. So, first, you are going to reconceptualize your cycle, then you are going to equip yourself with everything you need to put that shift into action.

After you have identified everything, you need you are going to start building the necessary habits to help you change your cycles and respond to life in a more calm, intentional manner rather than one that is overwhelmed and anxious. Then, you are going to practice putting those skills to use in your life when you experience anxiety in any way whatsoever. You will continue this process for a while until it becomes easier and easier for you to enforce these new skills in your life.

After a while, your goal will largely be to stay committed to your practice while also taking the time to identify how you can apply your new skills to other areas of your life. The more you do this, the more emotionally intelligent you will become, which ultimately means that you will be able to navigate difficult emotions in a more intentional and meaningful manner. This way, you can start navigating all of your emotions with ease, which means that navigating anxiety will also become easier.

Lastly, you need to take the time to review your process and see how it is working. At this point, you need to address your anxiety and consider how much you are still experiencing and how much that anxiety is continuing to affect you in your life. If you find that it is still affecting you in a large way, you are going to need to take the time to understand how and why and identify new ways for you to improve your resiliency and overcome your anxiety. If you find that you are managing it better and that it is starting to go away or become less problematic, then you can continue using the same strategies you have been enforcing all along.

Challenges You Might Face Along the Way

It is important to understand that even when you are in treatment to make something better, it does not necessarily mean that said thing is going to get all the way better right away. You might find that you struggle to get better at first because you are exposing yourself to things that are challenging and unusual for you, and this makes you feel uncomfortable and disconnected from your ability to feel safe. You may, at times, wonder why you are doing what you are doing and what benefit you are gaining from it or even wonder if your CBT is working at all. This is normal, and it will get better as time goes on. The more you commit to working on your skills and applying them to your anxious situations, the more improvement you will see.

With that being said, many people who enter CBT find themselves feeling nervous for many reasons beyond the initial anxiety that caused them to start seeking treatment in the first place. One common anxiety is that they do not know what life is going to look like when they are no longer worried, and so they become anxious and worried about the future. They may fear that there is no hope for a future without this particular anxiety or that if the anxiety does go away, they will feel overwhelmed and anxious by the amount of "free space" in their mind. Despite how strange this may feel to say out loud, this fear is actually incredibly normal and does begin to dissipate the more you continue practicing your CBT practices.

Another fear many people have is the fear around how they are going to face the challenges that they are trying to overcome. They begin to worry that they will not be able to face the challenges and overwhelm and that they are going to experience massive trauma if they even try, which can lead to many people becoming unwilling to face their fears. This anxiety is completely natural and normal and does get better as people find themselves dealing with their anxieties and triggers much better. Understand that until now you have trained yourself, or have been trained by your traumas, to avoid the trigger at all costs, so the idea of facing it on purpose seems silly and scary in a big way. However, I also understand that facing it on purpose is the only way that you can stay in control when you face it because you get to decide how much you face at once, and when. This means that you can prepare yourself for it, and gradually increase your exposure on purpose in a way that allows you to feel more and more in control as you continue to increase your exposure. Eventually, you will find yourself exposing yourself to the thing that made you so afraid with ease, and you will no longer have so much anxiety around that particular thing.

The last thing you might face that you need to be aware of are backslides. Many people who are working on healing themselves from anxiety find that they go through periods where they are doing great and periods where they are not. If you find yourself going through a period where you are not doing so great, you might find yourself feeling anxious and uncomfortable and worrying that you have a major setback. This particular fear is incredibly common with anxiety and can lead you to believe that you are doing something incredibly wrong and that you are not going to be able to rectify it. Trust that unless your reviews state that you truly are not improving, chances are these backslides are completely natural and are just a symptom of your healing from anxiety. Understand that in many cases, anxiety is caused by many things and complicates many areas of your life, which means you could have several triggers that are actively causing you to feel out of sorts. You might find that you drastically improve your responses to most triggers in most conditions, but that occasionally, a trigger or an experience catches you by surprise and leads to you feeling anxious all over again. This does not mean you are failing, and it simply means you are learning how to grow and that you need to practice using your skills in those particular circumstances, too. Over time, you will become a lot stronger with navigating your anxiety, and you will find that even more troubling experiences are not nearly as challenging.

Chapter 6: Applying Cognitive Behavioral Therapy to Your Anxiety

Now that you have come to understand how CBT works for anxiety in general, and for anxiety, it is time for you to start applying CBT to *your* anxiety. This is the point where we are going to sit with your anxious experiences and map out your present cycles so that you can understand how your anxiety is affecting you and what is likely causing it. You will become incredibly clear on what cycles you are facing, what the elements of those cycles are, and how they are impacting your wellbeing.

Once you understand the cycle, you are going through, and what is contributing to your anxiety, we are going to move on to identifying what exactly can be changed in your cycle, how you can change it, and what new practices you need to try. We are going to focus on how you can build these new practices and skills into your life so that you can begin to feel confident in them and recognize how they can support you in navigating your anxiety in a more effective manner. Then, you are going to start actually applying these skills to situations where you begin to experience anxiety.

After you begin applying those skills, we are going to focus on practices you can use to help you reinforce those new techniques and make sure that they really "take hold" on you and help you create the level of relief that you need. Then, you are going to learn about how you can stay committed to these practices even after you begin to see results, or when staying committed does not feel nearly as easy as it usually does.

Finally, you are going to move into reviewing your process and identifying where you are doing well and where you can improve your CBT approach to ensure that you are getting the most benefit out of it that you possibly can. The goal is to make sure that you not only experience some relief but ideally complete relief from your anxiety so that you no longer have to worry about dealing with your anxiety any more. This way, you do not have to feel anxious or worried that your symptoms are going to creep back in and cause problems at any point now or in the future, which means that you can confidently go back to living your life without concern.

As you go through the process outlined in this chapter, understand that it can take some time. The average CBT therapy lasts 6-20 sessions, with sessions being held every single week. This means that it could take you anywhere from 6-20 weeks to begin seeing the level of change and significance that you desire to see to help you recognize that the change you are creating is lasting and meaningful. Do not be afraid if you do not see a change immediately, and do not hesitate to linger in this chapter for as long as you need to until you start seeing the results. Ideally, you should take your time to give yourself the space to navigate these different aspects of your therapy with completion. With that being said, do not give yourself so much space that you begin to avoid dealing with your anxiety and navigating your triggers. If you find yourself engaging in avoidance, you are going to miss out on the benefits of CBT completely because you will never actually get into it enough to see any significant results.

Step 1: Assessment: Mapping Out Your Old Cycle

The first step in applying CBT to your anxiety disorder recognizes what your present cycles are and how they are negatively implicating your life. At this point, you need to assess your life to understand what you are doing, how your cycles are presently affecting your way of life, and what you can witness within yourself.This part of the CBT process requires deep self-awareness, so if you do not yet have a strong sense of self-awareness, you are going to need to begin practicing self-awareness in order to fulfill this step effectively. Fortunately, you can practice self-awareness and conduct your assessment all at the same time, so you do not have to worry about putting anything off or holding back if you find yourself struggling with self-awareness right now.

To begin mapping out your current anxiety cycle, you need to start honestly considering areas of your life where you experience anxiety and assessing them as thoroughly as you possibly can. In sessions, this often involves writing down the problem that leads you to believe that you have anxiety in the first place, then identifying what happens around that particular problem that leads to the occurrence in the first place.

For example, let's say you have panic attacks on a regular basis, and you have come to realize that they are problematic. You would begin your assessment by acknowledging that you have panic attacks and that they are causing problems for you in your everyday life. Then, you would go on to investigate what might be causing you to have these panic attacks and what these panic attacks are leading to afterward. At this point, you will likely be able to identify a specific trigger that is causing you to have panic attacks. Then, you might recognize that after your panic attacks, you feel even more afraid of that trigger because of how intensely you responded to it.

After you have identified the general cycle that exists around your anxiety, you need to go even deeper to allow yourself to find out exactly what your panic attacks entail and what symptoms the trigger, and attacks, are leading to in your life. At this point, you will want to pay close attention to what thoughts and feelings you have in your mind, body, and emotions at the time of the trigger, during the panic attack, and after the panic attack has subsided. You should also assess how you feel about the trigger well after the panic attack is over so that you can understand how your anxiety is affecting you around the topic of your trigger altogether.

After you have spent time recognizing what trigger is causing your anxiety, what anxious symptoms you are having after the trigger has been set off, and what you are experiencing after, you need to map everything out in plain order. This means that you need to look at the cycle objectively and write it out from point A to point B so that you can clearly understand what is happening within you, and outside of you, that is causing you to get this far into your anxiety.

There are two benefits you are going to gain from having your entire present anxiety cycle clearly mapped out. The first thing you will gain is awareness around what your anxiety looks and feels like, which can often be used to help minimize the intensity of anxiety attacks as they occur. When you are dealing with an anxiety attack in the active moment, it can feel overwhelming and unstoppable, and every symptom and new phase may seem scarier and scarier. However, when you can look at your typical cycle and rationally identify each point on the cycle and see yourself as falling in alignment with that particular cycle, it becomes easier for you to recognize that your symptoms are of anxiety. This way, you can at least stop believing that every thought you are presently having is true and that you are ultimately doomed or that there is no end to this overwhelming feeling.

The second thing you gain from having your entire anxiety cycle clearly mapped out is the opportunity to see where you are presently struggling with dealing with anxiety in the first place. Once you can spot all of the areas of weakness in your cycle, you can begin to identify what new skills you need to engage with in order to help you actually move through your anxiety with greater intention and strength in the future. As you begin to build these necessary skills, you will find yourself having far more success with navigating your anxiety in the future, which means that you will not be so trapped in the overwhelming cycle of anxiety anymore.

Step 2: Reconceptualization: Pinpointing Your Exact Problems

Now that you have successfully identified what your cycle looks like, you can begin the reconceptualization part of the process. This is where you identify your problematic thoughts and behaviors that are leading to unwanted feelings within your mind, emotions, and body. When you can identify your problematic thoughts, you can then reconceptualize this part of your cycle to begin identifying new skills and strategies you can try to break up the existing cycle that you have found yourself stuck in. This part of the process is important, as this is where you are going to create a plan for yourself so that you know and understand how you are going to be facing your anxiety in the future. With anxiety, especially, not having a plan can leave you feeling overwhelmed as you attempt to rely on strategies without any clear understanding of how they are meant to work or what they are meant to do for you. As a result, you will likely find yourself feeling completely out of sorts and unable to apply your new skills and strategies to your anxiety because the overwhelming energy and emotions become too much for you to handle.

Creating your plan for how you are going to proceed with your CBT requires you to do two things: spot problem areas in your cycle, and identify how you could go about those things differently to avoid having such an intense anxiety flare-up. In both circumstances, you want to make sure that you are identifying your problematic area and choosing an ideal way of approaching it when you are not actively dealing with anxiety. If you are actively dealing with anxiety or any other overwhelming emotion, you might find yourself struggling to rationally look at your cycle and identify ways that you can improve it.

Now, upon looking at your cycle, you want to see if you can spot the exact moment that you begin to experience anxiety in response to your trigger. Often, this lies within the space of your perception, or how you perceive the trigger the moment you experience it. After you have identified where the anxiety starts, you need to start pinpointing areas in your cycle where your anxiety worsens. Chances are, especially early on, changing your perception is going to be fairly hard. For this reason, you want to equip yourself with the tools to change your perception *and* to deal with the anxiety that follows so that during the time where you are learning to change your perception, your anxiety is also improving.

After you have identified where and why your anxiety begins and worsens, you can start re-conceptualizing your cycle. This means that you want to start identifying what new cycle you could implement to avoid having to deal with so much problematic anxiety in your life. Ideally, you should be identifying new thoughts and beliefs you can instill, as well as new skills that you can implement that are going to help you overcome the symptoms of your anxiety more effectively in the future. If you are unsure of what alternative skills you could be applying to help you navigate your anxiety more effectively, read through Chapter 7 to identify CBT techniques that you can use to start reducing and controlling your anxiety more effectively right away.

Now that you have identified where the problem areas are in your cycle, and what you can do to improve these areas of your cycle with new skills, you need to take a moment to finalize your map. At this point, you want to take a look at what your brand new ideal cycle would look like from start to finish if you were to implement these new skills from the start.

For example, maybe you would recognize your trigger and feel anxiety, but you would navigate that anxiety more effectively. Maybe instead of finding yourself experiencing more anxiety, you would navigate that anxiety with mindfulness and find your way through it much faster, which would result in zero waves of panic. Or, maybe you would find yourself not even reacting with anxiety anymore at all because you have mastered your skills so much that you are completely unphased by your previous trigger.

Step 3: Skill Acquisition: Building the Necessary Skills

At this point, you need to start focusing on building the necessary skills to help you overcome the anxiety that you have been facing. You should have a clear understanding of what skills you need, so now you are going to want to start focusing on how you can build those skills in your life. This part of the process is often done in an indirect manner so that individuals can focus on building and reinforcing their skills before they move on to actually applying them to their anxiety. Taking it slow and learning your skills first then applying them later is important because it gives you the opportunity to make sure that you are confident and comfortable in your new skills before you begin applying them to a high stakes experience. If you find yourself feeling too anxious or overwhelmed while also trying to learn a brand new skill, you will likely find yourself massively struggling and feeling completely out of sorts with yourself. It will be much easier to apply your skills to your anxiety cycle after you have already become familiar and comfortable with them. With that being said, you can certainly become mindful about *trying* to navigate your anxiety with these new skills right away, but do not put too much pressure on yourself as you do not want to develop a negative perspective on yourself and your ability to overcome your anxiety.

As you begin building the necessary skills, give yourself time to navigate each one before moving on to the next one to ensure that you can really begin strengthening your capacity to engage in each skill. Understand that these skills are often being used to rewire your brain from one that is naturally more anxious and worried to one that is naturally calmer and collected. For this reason, you want to make sure that you are being patient with yourself and giving your brain time to "rewire" which will ensure that you are able to begin getting the results that you desire from your sessions. At this point, if you do choose to apply your new skills and strategies toward your anxiety, take the pressure off completely by not allowing this time to count toward you working toward actually achieving your goal of minimizing your anxiety. You will not want to begin applying your new skills toward your goals until you are feeling far more confident in them so that you can engage in them in a more meaningful and intentional manner. This way, you do not overwhelm yourself too much by attempting to try something brand new to you during an emotionally overwhelming period of time.

Step 4: Skill Application: Applying Your Skills to Your New Cycle Strategy

Once you begin feeling confident in your new skills and are completely aware of how they work and what they feel like, you can begin applying them to your anxiety cycle with the intention of actually having an impact on overcoming your anxiety. At this point, you are actually going to be focusing on interrupting your anxiety cycle and infusing it with more calmness and control so that you are less likely to be emotionally hijacked by your anxiety.

Understand that the first few times you apply your new skills to your anxiety; it is going to feel overwhelming and challenging. It will not feel as simple as it did when you were practicing these skills outside of anxiety, which can make it feel like you are not making any progress *or* like you are not good enough at these skills just yet. This is a normal experience and response to trying something new during an emotionally charged time, so do not take it to mean that you are failing or that you are not having a positive impact on your ability to overcome your anxiety.

Once you start getting used to applying your skills to your anxious moments, it becomes easier for you to become less overwhelmed by applying these new skills to such emotionally charged situations. As a result, you will begin to start recognizing some improvements in your ability to navigate your anxiety more effectively.

It is important that during this phase, you document every experience you have with anxiety in a journal so that you can keep track of what you did and whether or not it worked. Tracking your experiences is going to allow you to see if your skills are supporting you in improving your anxiety or if you need to do something else to help you improve your anxiety even further.

The best way to track your experiences is to start documenting each individual anxiety cycle as you go through it so that you can identify what changed and what stayed the same. Make sure that you also reflect on how you felt about the experience *and* how you felt about the strategies and skills that you used to try to overcome your anxiety. This way, you can have a clearer understanding as to how you are navigating your anxiety and what can be done to improve your navigations over time, too.

Step 5: Skill Consolidation: Reinforcing New CBT Techniques

As you continue applying your new skills to your anxiety cycles, you want to focus on consolidating those skills so that they can become even more effective. This essentially means that you are going to identify how each skill can play together to minimize your anxiety while also turning these skills into new habits. When your new anxiety management skills become habitual, it becomes easier for you to navigate your anxiety each time going forward because you do not have to work so hard to remember what to do, how to do it, and when to do it.

Creating your new skills into habits is a way of consolidating this experience and information in your brain so that you can actually begin to change the way your brain is wired. This way, rather than automatically or habitually responding to your triggers with anxiety, you will begin to automatically and habitually respond to your triggers intentionally.

According to various scientific studies, habits take at least 30 days to begin actually wiring into your brain and becoming automatic processes, and it can take even longer when you are building new habits around emotionally charged circumstances. It is important that you continue to respond to your anxiety with your new skills over and over again, even if you feel like it is not working or like it is a chore every single time you try. The more you can continue to respond intentionally, the more effective it will be, and the more you will find yourself actually experiencing a massive change to the way that you navigate your anxiety.

It is important to understand that, especially with something as emotionally charged as anxiety, it can be easy to want to avoid your anxiety altogether and therefore avoid your new skills, too. As well, it can be challenging to override your automatic responses with intentional ones and truly see them all the way through. For that reason, you need to be patient with yourself and continue engaging in these new habits no matter what. The more you engage in them, the easier it will become and the more your anxiety is going to begin to subside as you learn how to respond to things that stimulate your anxiety with greater intention and mindfulness.

If you find that you are facing something that brings you massive amounts of anxiety, you might benefit from choosing to create and implement new habits one at a time rather than trying to create and implement new habits all at once. This way, you are able to easily focus on the way you feel and the goals you have along the way, rather than trying to focus on doing several different things at once. If this is the case, you want to focus on building the skill that is going to have the biggest impact on helping you control your anxiety first. Ideally, this should be something like a calming skill that helps you relax your nerves and ease into your emotional control once again. A breathing practice, journaling practice, meditation practice, or mindfulness practice would all serve well as this gives you something that you can begin using immediately upon recognizing that your anxiety has been triggered. These types of practices can be continually used at any point throughout your anxious episode, which means that you can continue using them over and over again until you begin to see results. Once you start feeling your anxiety coming under control, you can begin to enforce new skills in your life to help you begin overcoming even more of your anxiety episodes. Sometimes taking your time this way may make it feel like it takes much longer to overcome your anxiety altogether, but the process of taking your time during the approach actually helps you navigate your anxiety much easier in the long run. This way, you are less likely to overwhelm yourself and make even more traumatic experiences, which could make it even more challenging for you to overcome your anxiety in the long run.

Step 6: Generalization and Maintenance: Staying Committed to Your Practice

At this point, you already have a strong understanding of what your anxiety is caused by and why you are having such a hard experience with it. You have also had plenty of practice in enforcing your new skills toward your anxiety loop, and you might even find yourself experiencing great relief from your anxiety. As well, we have spoken plenty about how habits are formed and why you need to continually practice your new anxiety managing skills so that you can continue to form habits around your new skills. With that being said, it is important to understand that this habit part plays into the importance of you being able to maintain your lowered anxiety as much as it helps you actually overcome your anxiety in the first place.

It is important to understand that once you start seeing results and feeling more relaxed, it can be easy for old patterns to strike up again. Many people find themselves experiencing complete relief, only to "fall off the wagon," so to speak, and find themselves feeling overwhelmed all over again. This is because people do not realize that your old habits can easily rear their heads again and make themselves known. Your brain may be automatically responding with new habits, but it can be a delicate time as you can still just as easily fall into old habits again also, which can worsen your anxiety even more.

If you find yourself at a point where you are no longer feeling overwhelmed by your anxiety, and instead, you are starting to feel in control, then you need to take the time to actually make sure that you are *still* using your new skills. You should also continue monitoring yourself and periodically checking in on your improvements to make sure that you are still navigating your anxiety more effectively.

If you allow yourself to become complacent, that is when old habits have the easy opportunity to come back into existence and pull you off of your growth game. As a result, you are more likely to find yourself slipping back into old habits and feeling anxious all over again.

It is important to note that if you do accidentally allow yourself to fall back into old patterns and find your way back into your anxiety, this does not mean all of your efforts were lost. The new neuropathways you created through developing your new skills and habits still exist and can still be used to help you get right back on track again, even if you find yourself struggling and backsliding. Simply start mindfully practicing your new habits again right away, and you will find yourself quickly coming back into a state of calmness and being able to overcome your anxiety altogether.

Step 7: Post-Treatment Assessment: Reviewing Your Process and Growth

Now, we are going to dig into the importance of those journal trackers that we were talking about earlier on where you were told to track your progress and write down each new cycle as you went through it. At this point, you need to take the time to actually review those trackers and make sure that you are seeing the level of improvement that you want to be seeing. Taking the time to check-in and review your growth will ensure that you are creating the right changes in your cycle to help you truly overcome your anxiety and grow forward. This way, you can feel confident that your anxiety is going to be healed and that you are not going to face incredible bouts of anxiety going forward.

If you look through your reviews and you realize that you do not see significant improvements in your anxiety, you are going to want to stop and review your cycles and patterns to see if there is anything else you can do to help yourself improve. You might find that you simply need to keep practicing and reinforcing your new skills, or you might find that there are other skills you can begin implementing to help you improve even further.

It is important to understand that taking this time to review your anxiety practices is going to take you a lot further in your ability to overcome your anxiety. The more you can work toward creating a

strong plan for how you can overcome your anxiety, the better
your ability to overcome it will be.

Chapter 7: Cognitive Behavioral Therapy Techniques

When it comes to CBT, there are many techniques that you can use that will help you begin to create healing within yourself so that you can overcome your anxiety. Of those techniques, eight of them work incredibly well in helping you overcome anxiety in a profound and powerful manner. These eight include journaling, cognitive restructuring, exposure and response prevention, rescripting, progressive muscle relaxation, relaxed breathing, talking to a loved one, and physical exercise. All eight of these will support you with overcoming anxiety and healing yourself from troubling symptoms that anxiety may have caused in your life.

It is important to understand that many of these practices can be done during active bouts of anxiety, as well as in-between active bouts of anxiety to help keep you grounded and balanced. The more you can engage in these practices, the more you are going to find yourself reinforcing your habits and improving your skills, which will ultimately help you heal yourself from the troubles that you might face in your day to day life.

Cultivating a calmer and more peaceful life, in general, can also help reduce anxiety, as well as the impact anxiety has on you, by giving you the opportunity to overcome the stress in between your anxious periods. As a result, you are more likely to experience more peace in your life, too.

Journaling

Journaling can be used in two ways to help you when it comes to CBT. The first way is through simply journaling in a brain-dump format where you write down everything you are thinking about and all of the thoughts and feelings you are having so that you can get them out of your mind. The more you can write about when you are engaging in this type of journaling, the more you are getting out of your mind, and therefore the better you are going to feel. This can be incredibly helpful in supporting you with overcoming any form of anxiety that you may be dealing with as it allows you to get your worries out of your mind and let them go.

The other type of journaling that you can do that will be both supportive of helping you get things off your mind while also allowing you to organize your thoughts and track your experiences is called dysfunctional thought journaling. Some people also call this keeping a dysfunctional thought record.

Your dysfunctional thought record should have seven columns drawn onto a piece of paper so that you can write down seven pieces of information each time you have a dysfunctional thought. In the first column on the far left, you want to write down the time and date of your dysfunctional thought. In the second, you want to write down what the situation was that lead to the dysfunctional thought. Write about this part in detail. In the third column, write about the automatic thought you had immediately after the situation transpired. In the fourth column, write about any emotions you experienced as a result of the situation and your automatic thought. In the fifth column, write down the dysfunctional thought itself. In the sixth column, write down alternative thoughts that you could think that would serve as a more positive and helpful alternative to the initial thought you had. In the seventh column, write down the outcome of the exercise or how it has helped you confront the negative thought. If the process of confronting and addressing the thought helped you feel better or change your belief, or at least decrease your troubling emotions, write that down, too. The more you can keep track of, the better.

Cognitive Distortions and Cognitive Restructuring

Your anxiety, along with everyone else's, is caused by what is known as a cognitive distortion. Cognitive distortions resemble the false or misleading thoughts you are having when you are experiencing anxiety. When you have cognitive distortion, it can lead to you having a false belief about everything going on around you, and that can lead to you experiencing increased anxiety. Learning how to identify these cognitive distortions can help you engage in what is known as cognitive restructuring.

Cognitive restructuring means that you are actually changing the way you are thinking, not just the content of your thoughts but the actual thoughts themselves. When you engage in cognitive restructuring, you want to start by writing down what you are thinking that is causing you to experience anxiety. Be as specific as you can about this thought so that you understand all aspects of the thought that is leading to you experiencing anxiety.

Once you have written that down, begin to write down any facts you can think of that contradict the thought that you are having. Doing this actually supports you in coming into the realization that your thoughts are not always an accurate reflection of your reality, and that you can change your thoughts so that you can view a more realistic perception of your reality. If your mind is overwhelmed with facts that are supporting that perception and reality, write those down first, too, so that you can understand the two different types of perceptions that you might experience in your life.
Once you have written down all of your facts, you want to write down your judgment about the thought you are having. More specifically, you want to write down whether it is based on evidence, or if you think it is based more on your opinion on the matter. If it is based on your opinion, then you can change your opinion. If it is based on facts, then you need to change your perception so that the experience itself is more manageable. Rarely is there a circumstance where the facts support a level of anxiety that is completely unmanageable by the person experiencing anxiety in their life.

Exposure and Response Prevention

Exposure and response prevention is a form of CBT practice that supports you in preparing yourself to face your triggers in a way that is not so entirely overwhelming for you. When you engage in exposure and response prevention, your goal is to gradually increase your exposure to your trigger until you are no longer afraid of being around your trigger. This way, you are able to actually build up your tolerance and neutralize your response to the very thing that has been causing you anxiety for so long.
This particular form of therapy only works if you are able to actually engage in exposing yourself to small and controlled amounts of your trigger while being able to effectively work through the anxious responses you have to those exposures. Generally, it is used anytime you find yourself compulsively

wanting to engage in something, but you want to refrain from actually engaging in these compulsions. In most cases, when it comes to anxiety disorders, engaging in those compulsions would lead to you experiencing anxiety and discomfort rather than feeling relief from it. Although your brain might tell you that you are feeling relieved, the truth is that it would be reinforcing the anxiety that leads to the compulsions in the first place.

Most often, exposure is combined with journaling so that you can write down about your thoughts and experiences and document your thoughts, allowing you to further work through the anxiety that you have been experiencing. The more you can engage in this work, the more you are going to find yourself experiencing freedom from your anxiety.

Rescripting and Playing the Script Until the End

Rescripting, and playing the script until the end, are ways that you can work through anxiety by taking control over the anxious thoughts that you are experiencing within your mind. Often, people find themselves experiencing anxious thoughts and struggling to find ways to work through them. Rather than facing the thoughts and letting them play out, they avoid the thoughts and aggressively try to push them away out of their minds so that they can avoid experiencing such tremendous amounts of anxiety. The problem with pushing away or becoming afraid of your thoughts is that you are giving the thoughts more energy and attention than they need. As a result, they grow larger and feel even scarier, and you find yourself experiencing even more anxiety as a result.

If you allow your thoughts to happen naturally and you take a portion of control back, you allow yourself to step away from the anxious experience and instead regain control over your unwanted experience. This can help you begin to experience freedom from your anxiety in a far more positive manner. Using this strategy, you can not only put an end to your anxiety, but you can also put an end to the anxiety that you have about having anxiety, which is often caused by being too afraid to go through the motions of anxiety again.

Actually, engaging in these practices requires you to do two things. For rescripting, you want to take your time and identify what your thoughts are and why they are not serving you. Then, you want to start telling your story differently. Rescripting helps you change the course of your thoughts by changing the way your emotions are being felt and observed by your conscious mind. As a result, your emotions may go from feeling overwhelming and scary to feeling reasonable and understood. The more you can lead to you feeling reasonable and understanding, the more you are going to be able to help yourself to improve your response to anxiety.

When you play the script until the end, you can engage in rescripting at the same time. However, the goal here is also to understand how scary your thoughts actually are by allowing them to play all the way out until the end. Often, we get hung up on the scary part of thought, which results in us continually feeling as though there is nothing we can do to feel better. If, however, we can recognize that we are getting hung up on these scary parts of the thoughts and we allow ourselves to keep thinking the thought through, then we can see that the thought itself is not entirely scary. You do this by asking yourself, "and then what?" until you reach a point in your reality where the scary or anxiety-inducing experience would no longer be such a big deal.

For example, let's say you are scared of public speaking because you are afraid that you will stumble over your words, and people will look at you funny. If you keep getting hung up on this part of the experience, then you might grow incredibly afraid of public speaking to the point that you want to cancel your public speaking engagement. If, however, you instead begin to ask yourself "and then what?" you can start to become aware of what might happen if you were to stumble on your words, and people looked at you funny. Perhaps you would acknowledge that you would keep speaking, and then you would finish the speech and be done. Or, maybe you would acknowledge that you feel embarrassed, take a breath, and keep going. Whatever the script looks like for you, keep seeing it through until you are at the end so that you are more likely to get to the point where you recognize that no matter what happens, it's not the end of the world.

Progressive Muscle Relaxation

Progressive muscle relaxation, sometimes called PMR, is a type of treatment that aligns with meditation and relaxation in one and actually supports people in bringing peace into their body. For people who are experiencing anxiety, PMR can help you release the tension and tightness that you are carrying within your body so that you can begin to feel more at peace. This gives your body the biofeedback of "I'm okay," which leads to your anxiety gradually reducing until the point where it is no longer existent.

You can engage in PMR by essentially focusing on one area of your body at a time and instructing that area of your body to relax. To engage in proper PMR, you want to focus on starting at either your feet or your head, and you want to instruct every major muscle group on the way to your head or your feet to relax. The more you can do this, the more you are going to find yourself experiencing freedom from the tightness and anxiety that you are carrying within your body.

PMR can be done anytime you are experiencing nerves or a busy mind, and it can also be done as a part of a habitual routine to help you release daily stress and anxiety, which is especially important if you are experiencing a generalized anxiety disorder. You can easily engage in PMR on your own, or you can follow a recorded meditation that guides you through PMR if you would like some assistance in navigating this particular relaxation method.

Relaxed Breathing

Relaxed breathing can help you literally breathe peace into your body by taking back control over your automatic responses and relaxing through them. When you are anxious, your body will immediately begin to tense up, and your breath will grow more shallow. You might even find yourself holding your breath if you are feeling particularly anxious, which can lead to even more challenging experiences. If you can take back control over your breath, you can begin to breathe in a deeper, calmer, and more relaxed manner that encourages your entire body to relax as deeply as possible.

Your relaxed breathing can be done on your own or following meditation or guided experience on the internet. These days, many devices like your phone or your smartwatch also have breathing apps built-in that can help you intentionally slow down your breath and bring calm back into your body. Following these tools can be extremely helpful in dissipating your anxiety and taking back control, especially if you find yourself experiencing constant and chronic anxiety. Often, seeing the app on your phone or smartwatch can actually trigger calmness, too, because you become so used to that particular tool being used to help slow your breath and calm you down.

If you want to do relaxed breathing on your own, you can simply remember an easy breathing rhythm and then intentionally practice that breathing rhythm for one entire minute, or until you begin to calm down, whichever comes last. A great and easy-to-remember breathing rhythm you can use when you are feeling anxious is to breathe in for five seconds, hold it for six seconds, and exhale for seven seconds. These numbers are simple to remember, and this rhythm will help you calm yourself down and begin to experience more peace within your body, mind, and emotions relatively quickly.

Talking to A Loved One

Your anxiety may be your own, but that does not mean that you have to face it alone. For many people, especially those who are facing intense or overwhelming anxiety, having the help of a loved one can be extremely supportive in enabling them to overcome their anxious experiences. You might find that the more you can surround yourself with the support and warmth of loved ones in your life, the more you are going to be able to heal yourself from having troubling anxiety. The reason behind this is that many people succumb to the stigma that anxiety is in any way bad or negative, and so they find themselves experiencing shame and guilt around their anxiety. As a result, they end up holding back and keeping their anxiety to themselves, which can lead to them having even more anxiety.

Suffering alone is not helpful, and it can also lead to you having even more challenging experiences. If, however, you take the time to identify who you can talk to that will be able to respect you and help you and you take the time to work toward actually reaching out to them when you are feeling anxious, you will find yourself feeling far more supported. This way, you no longer feel as though you have to go through anxiety alone, and both you and your support can help you begin to overcome your anxious experiences.

Physical Exercise

When you get anxious, your body produces a large amount of cortisol and adrenaline. Both of these are meant to stimulate enough energy for you to be able to engage in "fight or flight" as needed so that you can safely remove yourself from the situation that you have perceived to be dangerous. If you are not making use of this influx of energy, you will find yourself experiencing a sense of discomfort in your life because this energy can begin to become overwhelming. Rather than being adequately used, it becomes pent up, and you find yourself feeling worse and worse.

If you take the time to engage in physical exercise on a regular basis, it is going to do two things. First, it is going to help you move through that built up energy so that it does not sit there nagging at you and making you feel worse. If you are feeling incredibly anxious, rather than engaging in fight or flight, you can engage in some light cardio or even a more calming form of exercises like yoga or tai chi. Engaging in these types of exercises will help you immediately relieve yourself of the energy that you have built up within you as a result of your anxiety.

Aside from helping you relieve yourself from an immediate bout of anxiety, physical exercise is also going to support you with balancing your hormones and supporting your overall sense of wellbeing. People who exercise on a more regular basis find themselves feeling far more resilient to things like stress and overwhelm, which can be helpful in supporting you with navigating troubling and unwanted experiences with anxiety. This way, you are more likely to feel healthier and more at peace in between bouts of anxiety, and you are more likely to bounce back from your bouts of anxiety with greater ease.

Chapter 8: Monitoring Yourself for Consistent Improvements

As you continue to develop your CBT practice, you are going to want to make sure that you are monitoring yourself so that you can ensure that you see consistent improvements. In chapter 6, we talked about the post-treatment assessment, but now we are going to talk about how you can go even deeper into that post-treatment assessment. Engaging in a proper and thorough post-treatment assessment is important as it will ensure that you are making progress in the right direction. Make sure to follow these steps so that you can keep close track of your progress and support yourself in having the best results in overcoming your anxiety with CBT.

Tracking Your Progress in a Journal

In chapter 6, I mentioned the importance of tracking your progress in a journal, and I want to echo it again right now. Using a journal to track your progress with your anxiety is important as it is going to help you track how effectively you are actually navigating your anxiety each time you are faced with a new bout. Early on, your tracking journal is likely not going to show a lot of changes, although some people do recognize that they experience massive improvements from their anxiety fairly early on with CBT. With that being said, you want to keep track because often around the 4-6 week mark, you begin to see huge improvements in your ability to apply your skills and navigate your anxiety more effectively.

Tracking your progress in your journal should be done every single time you experience a bout of anxiety and use your new skills to navigate that bout of anxiety. This means that even if you are experiencing anxiety multiple times a day, you need to track every single bout so that you can clearly see how your skills are working. In some cases, you will see yourself improving over the course of a few hours, which can be incredible to watch. Often, the more you realize you are successfully navigating your anxiety, the easier it becomes to continue successfully navigating it going forward.

Having A Consistent Rating System

When you track your anxiety in a journal, it is important that you use the same tracking system over and over again. This way, you can clearly monitor your anxiety and get a true grasp of how well things are actually improving. If you are constantly attempting to track different variables, you are going to find yourself struggling to identify whether you are improving or not because you will not be able to determine if your symptoms are the same, worse, or better than the last time you experienced anxiety.

Your rating system should consistently track these variables:

- The time and date of your episode;
- What triggered your anxiety;
- What your automatic thought was;
- What your following behavior was;
- How you began to feel in your emotional body;
- How you began to feel in your physical body;
- What you are thinking and feeling during the peak of your anxiety;
- What you are thinking and feeling as the anxiety begins to subside;
- How long the episode lasted;
- What practices or skills you applied, when, and how well they worked;
- A detailed one-sentence description of the cycle you went through.

This may seem like a lot to track, but as you continue to track all of this information, you will come to realize that it is incredibly helpful to have it all on hand so that you can keep going through it and reviewing your progress over time.

Monitoring Your Progress Over Time

If you track your anxiety and your CBT practices properly, you should have plenty of "data" to reflect back on to let you know how well you are doing with navigating your anxiety or not. This way, you can start monitoring your progress over time to see how well you are doing and whether or not your skills are improving and working toward helping you overcome your anxiety.

Ideally, you should focus on reviewing your tracking journal every week so that you can see how you have improved over the week. This will help you identify any patterns, recognize areas of growth, and identify areas where you can improve your ability to overcome your anxiety so that you are more likely to move beyond it.

What to Do When You See Improvements

After you start to notice significant improvements in your anxiety, you might not want to keep track of your journal as often. With that being said, you should continue to write in and monitor your journal on a consistent basis until you reach the goal that you initially set out to achieve when you decided you wanted to treat your anxiety. Once you have achieved that goal, continue tracking and monitoring your improvements for another week or two to make sure that you are still doing well and that there are no unintentional backslides. This way, you are more likely to find your way to complete freedom without a relapse of your anxiety.

Once you feel absolutely confident that your anxiety has been dealt with and that you are no longer at risk of having it become so problematic anymore, you can stop tracking your anxiety in your journal. You can also stop doing official monitoring of your tracking since you will no longer be tracking any of the data relating to your anxiety.

With that being said, you should continue to engage in regular journaling, and through that, you can engage in a self-awareness monitoring practice on a fairly consistent basis. This self-awareness monitoring practice can be as simple as checking in with yourself and asking if you still feel as though you are navigating your anxiety effectively and without it leading to such overwhelming and unwanted problems. If you find yourself struggling once again, simply resume your previous CBT practices and tracking so that you can start finding your solution and resolving your anxiety all over again. This time around, it should be much simpler than the last since you have already built and consolidated your skills, and now you just need to focus on intentionally applying them to your anxiety once again.

Chapter 9: What to Do if it Doesn't Seem Like It's Working

If you begin engaging in CBT and it seems like things are not working, this can be fairly disconcerting. You might think that you are doing something wrong or that your anxiety is so bad that there is no chance that you could possibly experience any sense of relief from the anxiety that you are facing. Fortunately, that is unlikely to be the case, and there are various things you can do to try to help yourself experience greater relief from your anxiety and any symptoms that have been accompanying your anxiety.

How Can You Tell if it's Working or Not?

The first thing you need to do is honestly consider the fact that what might seem like it is not working is actually working, and you are just impatient toward the results. When you are experiencing anxiety, it can be challenging to identify whether or not you are actually getting better, especially if you are dealing with something that is particularly intense. Before you write CBT off as not working for you, it is important that you honestly assess if it is actually not working, or if you are struggling to be patient with it and yourself as you begin to train yourself to have healthier responses to your anxiety.

The easiest way for you to honestly assess whether your CBT is working or not is to consider how well you have been sticking to the practices, and how long you have been doing it for. If you have been doing CBT for some time, but you find that you are not consistent with practicing and implementing your skills, chances are the problem is not your CBT practice but your lack of consistency. Likewise, if you find that you have been keeping up with the practices, but you have not been doing them long, chances are you are being too impatient and not giving yourself enough time to start seeing your results. Being patient with yourself and giving your practice your full commitment are two important things that you need to try doing before you decide that your CBT is not working for you.

What to Do if You Do Not see Improvements

If you are consistent and you have been patient, but you do not see the results you desire from your CBT, there are a few things that you can consider trying. The first thing is assessing your reconceptualization process and making sure that you have identified the best skills for you to implement in order to help you overcome your anxiety. At this point, you may realize that there are more skills that you can use to support you in creating a stronger ability to manage your anxiety and overcome your anxious episodes. This way, you can start learning and implementing these new skills in a more effective manner.

When you reassess yourself and your anxiety cycle, it is important that you review what your present cycle is and start the entire CBT 7-step process over again. Chances are, at least, some of your efforts have paid off, and you are experiencing even small amounts of relief from your anxiety, which means that your cycle may have changed. Rediscovering your present cycle will ensure that you are able to recognize what can be done to help you navigate your anxiety more effectively for what it is now, rather than trying to navigate what you have already dealt with.

As you go through the process of reassessing and reconceptualizing your anxiety with CBT once again, make sure that you review what you have already been doing and how it has been working. If you find that some of your practices have already been working, you can keep using those practices to help you experience even more relief from your anxiety. If you find that some of them have not been working at all, you can either modify them or try something completely different to see if you can experience relief from a different approach.

When it comes to CBT, it can take a few tries sometimes to find what is going to work for you in overcoming your anxiety. Since each person's experience with anxiety can be so drastically different from everyone else's, there is no single clear route that can be taken, even with a practice like CBT. Although CBT will help make your experience more direct and clear, it may not give you all of the clarity and relief you need. Take your time and continue practicing until you find what works, and through that you will find yourself experiencing complete relief from your anxiety over time.

If you have continued trying and you have reassessed and reconceptualized your CBT approach a few times, yet you are still not experiencing the level of relief you want or need, you may need to combine CBT with another approach. Practicing CBT with a therapist to get more intensive support, or talking to your therapist about an alternative practice, you may be able to try can be helpful. Alternatively, you might consider using anti-anxiety medications to help you overcome your anxiety and find your way to feeling complete relief from anxiety. While medications are not needed for everyone, some people may need them to help them deal with overwhelming and problematic anxiety so that they are no longer being troubled with them. If you do find yourself using medication for anxiety, make sure that you continue to use CBT as well, as using both will help you have a well-rounded and complete approach that will support you in experiencing relief from all angles.

What to Do if You Are Feeling Worse

If you find that you experience anxiety, and despite your best efforts with CBT, you are feeling worse, you need to make sure that you enlist the support of a professional. Not all forms of anxiety can be self-managed, and continuing to live with unmanaged anxiety without any proper support can be overwhelming and even traumatizing. Seeking the support of a therapist and a professional doctor can support you in overcoming your anxiety. You might find that you need to take medications or use more intensive forms of therapy to help you overcome your anxiety.

In the process of seeking out professional support, you can continue practicing enforcing the skills of CBT. Even though it may not be providing you with any relief right now, the skills within CBT are incredibly helpful and will offer you emotional and cognitive support in other areas of your life as needed. If anything, CBT combined with another treatment will provide you with a more well-rounded approach to navigating and managing your anxiety effectively.

Chapter 10: Natural Ways to Manage Anxiety

One of the biggest benefits behind managing anxiety with CBT is that you are managing your anxiety in a natural way. While some forms of anxiety will require medication, some people find that creating a natural management plan is much easier and feels more aligned with them and their needs. With that being said, CBT is not the only way that you can manage your anxiety in a natural manner that will help improve your symptoms and support you with feeling your best. If you want to really approach your anxiety with a full system for helping you not only manage but also heal and cure your anxiety, incorporating some alternative natural approaches can be helpful, too.

When it comes to anxiety, specifically, there are several things you can do to help you begin to manage your anxiety more effectively. Most of these methods are lifestyle methods, although some of them can be targeted toward anxiety itself, too. The eight things that you can do that will really help you navigate your anxiety more effectively and naturally heal yourself include: exercise, avoiding anxiety-inducing substances, resting, meditating, improving your diet, teas, and herbs, aromatherapy, and taking the pressure off of yourself. In this chapter, we are going to talk about how you can engage in each of these things to support you in naturally relieving yourself from symptoms of anxiety.

Maintain Regular Exercise

Exercise is necessary for your general wellbeing, yet many people fail to incorporate enough exercise into their everyday routine. Ideally, you should be engaging in at least 30 minutes of moderate exercise every single day, as well as moving your body around at least once per hour. Ensuring that you engage in enough movement and exercise will help you use up any adrenaline and cortisol that your body may produce as a byproduct of your anxiety. As well, it will help naturally regulate your hormones and chemicals to ensure that your hormonal system is functioning more effectively. For some people, this can translate to experiencing less anxiety overall because their system functions more effectively as a result of their exercise.

In addition to helping you regulate your hormones and chemicals within your body, exercise can also release endorphins into your system that actually support you in staying more relaxed and navigating anxiety, as well as other emotions more effectively. These endorphins can be found in your body for up to several hours after working out, meaning that one single workout session can help regulate your hormones, chemicals, and emotions for several hours. If you continue working out on a consistent basis, this can translate to ongoing, long-term relief from your anxiety symptoms.

Avoid Alcohol, Cigarettes, and Caffeine

Alcohol is known for being a natural sedative, which means that it can support you with relaxing yourself from anxiety. One single glass of wine or a shot of whiskey can calm your nerves and support you with navigating your anxiety more effectively – at first. However, as soon as the buzz from that small portion of alcohol wears off, your anxiety can come back far stronger and more intense than ever. Attempting to treat your anxiety with alcohol can lead to alcoholism while also exacerbating the symptoms of your anxiety and making you feel even worse in the long run.

Cigarettes are also known for exacerbating your anxiety by worsening your risk of anxiety over time. Although smoking a cigarette when you are actively feeling stressed might seem to calm you down, the reality is that research has shown that long-term cigarette usage actually massively increases your risk for problematic anxiety symptoms. As well, nicotine itself is said to increase your anxiety symptoms, which means that you may actually find yourself feeling even worse after a cigarette.

Lastly, caffeine is known as a stimulant and can massively aggravate your anxiety. If you are drinking caffeine on a regular basis, and you find yourself dealing with problematic anxiety, you need to start cutting back on caffeine or eliminating it entirely. Releasing caffeine from your daily drinking ritual will massively support you with avoiding unwanted anxiety and allowing yourself to experience more calmness in your life.

Create A Stronger Rest Routine

People who experience chronic or problematic anxiety often report that they tend to experience a strange or inconsistent sleep schedule. For some people, the strange or inconsistent sleep schedule might be the result of their anxiety itself, whereas others might find that the schedule is more closely linked to their lifestyle and leads to the experience of anxiety. If you are trying to overcome anxiety in your life, learning how to navigate a healthier rest cycle will be important to your wellbeing. The more you can support yourself in navigating a healthier rest cycle, the more you will find yourself experiencing freedom from your anxiety.

Ideally, you should have a strong bedtime routine as well as plenty of sleep throughout each night to support you with experiencing healthier rest cycles and more support from your sleep. With both in place, you will likely find yourself experiencing significant relief from your anxiety.

For your bedtime routine, try avoiding using your phone, tablet, or any other device with a screen for at least 30-45 minutes before bed. As well, do not read or watch television in bed or otherwise engage in active activities in your bed as this can lead to you associating your bed with a space to be active and awake. You should also try incorporating some relaxing pre-bedtime routines, like drinking a relaxing tea, journaling, taking a warm bath, or doing a gentle yoga practice. These types of calming experiences will help you release your stress, calm your mind, and prepare yourself for a good night's sleep.

You should also make sure that you are going to bed at a reasonable hour and waking up 7-9 hours later, which is the recommended amount of sleep for the average adult. Getting a proper amount of sleep and waking up on time will ensure that you are well-rested when you wake up and that you have not overslept, too.

Practice Meditating

Meditation is one of the most powerful things you can do to help you naturally relieve anxiety, and it can also support you with active anxiety attacks or bouts of anxiety if you find yourself struggling. Having a regular meditation practice will support you with relaxing yourself in between anxiety, and with managing your anxiety more effectively and completely when it spikes. Your main goal with meditation is to relax your mind and let yourself experience peace, so naturally, this can have a positive and healthy impact on your mind, especially when you are navigating anxiety. In fact, some studies have shown that those who meditate on a consistent basis experience massive relief from things such as anxiety, stress, worry, and even depression and other emotional or mental disorders.

If you are new to meditation, getting into the practice of meditating for just 10-15 minutes per day can have a huge impact on helping you relieve yourself from anxiety. However, you should be focused on working your way up to meditating for about 30 minutes a day, as this is what John Hopkins medical research center recommends as being the best length of time for relief from anxiety, as well as depression. You should practice meditating whether you feel anxious or not, as keeping a healthy and ongoing meditation practice will support you in fully overcoming anxiety in the long run. Think of this as being similar to practicing CBT techniques outside of anxiety before bringing them into your anxiety cycle: the more you practice, the better you get, and the more effective it will be at helping you in your times of need.

If you struggle to meditate, following a guided meditation on YouTube can be helpful in allowing you to meditate more effectively. You may also want to turn meditation into more of a ritual where you involve gentle music, a comfortable pillow and blanket, and some soothing aromatherapy or candles to help set the tone. The more you can relax and let your mind experience relief, the more peace you will experience in your life.

Improve Your Diet

Much like alcohol, cigarettes, and caffeine can impact your anxiety, and your diet can actually impact your anxiety, too. Your diet can increase symptoms of anxiety in many ways. If you are not eating enough or you are not eating well enough, your body can become stressed from your unhealthy dietary styles and can actually increase your levels of cortisol in your body, which can lead to symptoms of anxiety. As well, some foods are naturally energizing and can lead to you having anxiety as a result of these boosted energies. Learning to avoid any form of natural stimulants can be helpful in supporting you with navigating your anxiety more effectively.

The foods you need to avoid include any that have been processed or that are laced in chemicals such as artificial flavors, colors, or preservatives. You also need to avoid letting your blood sugars drop too low or letting yourself get dehydrated, as these can both lead to the increase of anxiety within your body. In addition to that, avoid high sugar diets and stimulating foods and herbs like ginseng, chocolate (which can contain caffeine), and any other number of herbs or supplements that may be stimulating in nature.

Eating a diet that is healthy and rich in complex carbohydrates, vegetables, fruits, and lean proteins can help you support yourself with overcoming anxiety more effectively. You can also focus on eating foods that are known for supporting your brain health, such as those that are rich in fatty omega-3 acids, like fish, as these can support your brain is having an easier time creating new neural pathways. Some studies suggest that this may make it easier for you to be more resilient toward anxiety and more effective in implementing your new CBT practices.

Use Calming Teas and Herbs

Just like certain herbs can stimulate you, others can actually help you relax, too. Learning how to use tea and herbs to support you in relaxing yourself can be helpful in allowing you to bring down your energy levels and offset your anxiety naturally. Some people like to drink calming teas on a regular basis, whereas others might drink them exclusively around the time that they are feeling anxious so that they can experience relief. Ideally, you should drink calming teas on an ongoing basis. However, either method will support you in naturally bringing down your energy levels and calming yourself from anxiety.

There are seven incredible natural loose leaf teas you can use that will really help you when it comes to bringing down your anxiety levels. These seven include peppermint tea, chamomile tea, lemon balm tea, passionflower tea, green tea, rose tea, and lavender tea. Each of these is known for having various constituents in it that can help you naturally relieve yourself of anxiety, while often also supporting you in uplifting any depression that you may be experiencing.

When it comes to drinking teas or using herbs to support you in navigating anxiety, it is important that you are aware of which ones might worsen your symptoms. Many teas contain higher levels of caffeine, which may or may not offset your anxiety. Some people can handle lightly caffeinated teas, whereas other people might find themselves feeling far too sensitive to even small amounts of caffeine. You can test to see where you fall on this scale. With that being said, avoid black teas and Pu-erh teas as they are known for having more caffeine than coffee, which can make them terrible for managing anxiety. White tea, mate, green tea, and oolong tea can all be used instead of caffeinated beverages and may be gentle enough that they do not stimulate your anxiety, but they do give you a slight boost in energy.

Try Aromatherapy

Aromatherapy has been said to be a powerful tool for helping navigate many different ailments, including anxiety. If you are experiencing troubling anxiety, using aromatherapy may help you support yourself in lowering your anxiety levels and supporting yourself with feeling more at peace in your life. When using aromatherapy, there are a few things that you should know to make sure that you get the most out of your experience while also staying safe.

The first thing you need to know is that aromatherapy works on two levels. The first level is by infusing the constituents of the oil with your body, meaning that it works similarly to tea. The same way that certain elements of tea encourage you to relax in the way that certain elements of aromatherapy blends will encourage you to relax, too. The other way that aromatherapy can help you is through olfaction. Olfaction is a process whereby you smell something, and it activates a part of your limbic system, which essentially means that it triggers certain memories. When certain aromatherapy blends have the capacity to activate your more peaceful memories, it can support you with navigating anxiety more effectively.

Before you begin using aromatherapy, make sure that you purchase your oils from a high-quality source that you trust completely. As well, make sure that you are aware of what oils are safe and are not safe for you to use. Sometimes, essential oils can be dangerous for certain people with certain conditions or for pets, so you need to make sure that the oils you use are safe for yourself and everyone in your home. If you find that the oil you want to use is not safe, do not use it at all as it can cause problems for you or the members of your family rather quickly.

The oils that you can consider using to support you with navigating anxiety include lavender oil, rose oil, vetiver oil, ylang-ylang oil, frankincense oil, geranium oil, jasmine oil, and chamomile oil. All eight of these are known for supporting people with reducing their symptoms of anxiety and experiencing greater calm and peace in their lives.

Release the Pressure From Yourself

The last and sometimes most powerful thing you can do for yourself when you are dealing with anxiety and trying to overcome it naturally releases the pressure for yourself. As a species, we have a tendency to put a massive amount of pressure on ourselves through the expectations that we tend to have on ourselves in life. You may be combining your own high expectations with the expectations that other people have of you, leading to you overwhelming yourself with expectations that you cannot meet. If you are overwhelmed by the expectations that you have placed on yourself, or that you feel others have placed on you, you need to practice taking the pressure off and giving yourself space for a while.

Releasing the pressure from yourself can be difficult, especially if you have had high expectations of yourself for quite some time. You might find yourself struggling to fully release the pressure and let yourself be patient and gentle with yourself, even if you have set the intention to do so. In this case, exercising the practice of CBT on your tendency to put pressure on yourself may be ideal as you learn to change your perspective and give yourself permission to slow down in life and take some of the stuff off of your plate.

The more you can be gentle and patient with yourself, the more you are going to find yourself experiencing peace from your anxiety. Many people are surprised to learn that when they stop expecting so much of themselves, suddenly they have a lot more energy to get everything done. Expectations themselves have a way of slowing people down and making them feel exhausted. If you never take the time to address this, you are going to find yourself constantly feeling overwhelmed and overworked. Learn to take the pressure off of yourself and give yourself permission to take it easy. Book time off, stop saying yes to everything, and delegate some of your tasks so that you do not have to attempt to do so much by yourself. The more you can work on navigating things in a less stressful manner, the less pressure you are going to feel, and therefore the less anxiety you are likely going to feel, too.

Conclusion

Navigating anxiety can be a tricky thing, especially if you are not particularly used to navigating something as intense and overwhelming as anxiety. When it comes to anxiety, the fewer skills you have in managing your emotions and your stress levels, the harder it becomes. With that being said, even people who have strong coping skills often find themselves massively struggling with anxiety and feeling completely overwhelmed by their symptoms. Anxiety itself has a way of being incredibly overpowering and emotionally hijacking people when they are least expecting it.

Learning how to navigate your anxiety may seem challenging, but if you want to recover a natural and comfortable way of living, you need to get it under control. Living with unmanaged anxiety can lead to major disturbances in your day to day life, which is never enjoyable. Not to mention, anxiety can also lead to people experiencing heightened stress levels, which can lead to troubles like depression, digestive disorders, and even heart problems due to the immense strain stress and anxiety put on your body.
I hope that in reading this book, you have come to understand one of the most powerful natural methods you can use for actually curing your anxiety. CBT not only gives you tools to navigate your anxiety but also lays the framework for you to be able to overcome your anxiety altogether completely. By changing the way you think and process thoughts, you change the way you feel and ultimately regain control over yourself while having the capacity to overcome your anxiety fully.

As you continue forward after reading this book, I encourage you to take your time and really place your focus on your ability to overcome anxiety in your life. You need to make sure that you continue to feel empowered to make a change in your life and that you continue to engage in your new skills even if it seems like your new skills are not working. Continue applying them, and continue assessing yourself to see how you are really doing. If you really feel like nothing is changing, make sure that you address this and either adjust your approach or incorporate more healing methods to help you overcome your anxiety.

At the end of the day, anxiety is troublesome, but it is not something that you need to be afraid of for the rest of your life. While it may feel like anxiety is ruling your life right now, it does not have to be this way forever. You can overcome your anxiety and find your way to peace if you allow yourself the opportunity to continue practicing these methods every single day, and you keep an open mind. The more you can stay receptive to the possibility of there being a life beyond anxiety, the more likely you will be to experience one.

Lastly, if you read *Cognitive Behavioral Therapy for Anxiety: Master, the Negative Voice in Your Head, Change Negative Thoughts, Emotions, and Bad Behaviors, Reduce Stress and Anger Management to Overcome Anxiety* and felt that it supported you in understanding and navigating your anxiety more effectively, I ask that you, please take the time to review it on Amazon Kindle. Your honest feedback would be greatly appreciated, as it will help me create more great books for you while also helping others who are also suffering from anxiety discover a great resource that can hopefully support them in overcoming their troubles, too.

Thank you, and best of luck in changing your mind, and in changing your life.

PS. If you are looking for additional ways to master your emotions and heal your life, my books Cognitive Behavioral Therapy for Depression, Emotional Intelligence for Self-Discipline *and* Emotional Intelligence for Leaders *are great resources that you might enjoy.*

9 781653 655571